Chapter Summary

Introduction

Achieving financial freedom is a goal that many people aspire to, but it can be challenging to know where to start. However, one of the best ways to begin is by saving money and investing it wisely. This approach can help you build wealth and achieve financial independence over time. In this book, we will explore the best strategies for saving money and investing in the future.

To begin, we will cover budgeting, which is the cornerstone of any successful financial plan. Budgeting allows you to track your income and expenses, so you can identify areas where you can save money. We'll provide you with practical tips for creating a budget that works for your lifestyle and financial goals.

Debt reduction is another essential topic that we will discuss. Debt can be a significant obstacle to achieving financial freedom, as it can limit your ability to save and invest. We will provide you with strategies for reducing and managing debt, so you can free up more money to put towards your financial goals.

We'll also explore emergency funds, which are crucial for protecting yourself against unexpected expenses or financial emergencies. Having an emergency fund can help you avoid taking on debt or dipping into your savings, allowing you to stay on track with your long-term financial goals.

When it comes to investing, we'll cover different types of investments, including real estate, gold, silver, stocks, bonds, and other financial assets. We'll explain the pros and cons of each investment type, so you can make informed decisions about where to invest your money.

Additionally, we'll provide you with tips for using your investments to buy assets that can generate passive income, such as rental properties or dividend-paying stocks. This approach can help you build wealth over time and achieve financial independence.

Overall, this book will provide you with the knowledge and tools you need to save money, reduce debt, build an emergency fund, and invest in the future. By following these strategies, you can achieve your financial goals and enjoy the freedom that comes with financial independence.

Chapter 1: The Importance of Saving Money

Saving money is a fundamental financial skill that everyone should develop. It involves setting aside some portion of your income for future use rather than spending it all at once. Saving money can provide a sense of financial security, help you achieve your financial goals, and ensure that you have a comfortable life in the future. In this detailed response, we will explore the importance of saving money and how it can benefit you in different aspects of your life.

1. Emergency fund

An emergency fund is a crucial aspect of personal finance, and it's essentially a savings account that is set aside for unexpected expenses such as medical bills, car repairs, and job loss. Emergencies can occur at any time, and having an emergency fund can help you avoid going into debt or dipping into your other savings accounts, such as your retirement savings account, to cover these expenses. Therefore, saving money can help you build a safety net that can protect you and your family from financial hardship during unexpected times.

2.   Achieving financial goals

Saving money is also an essential aspect of achieving your financial goals. Whether you want to buy a house, a car, go on a vacation, or retire comfortably, saving money is the first step towards achieving these goals. By setting up a budget and saving a portion of your income, you can create a plan that helps you achieve your financial objectives. By saving money, you can also ensure that you don't have to rely on credit cards or loans to finance your goals, which can save you money on interest payments in the long run.

3.   Retirement savings

Saving money is critical for your retirement as well. As people are living longer and healthcare costs are rising, it's important to save money to ensure that you have a comfortable retirement. By contributing to a retirement savings account, such as a 401(k) or an Individual Retirement Account (IRA), you can ensure that you have enough money to sustain yourself in retirement. Moreover, saving money early in your career can lead to significant benefits through compound interest.

4   Financial freedom

Saving money can also provide you with a sense of financial freedom. When you save money, you have the flexibility to make choices that align with your values and goals, rather than being forced to take the first available opportunity that comes your way. Having savings can also help you start a business, change careers, or take a break from work without worrying about your finances. By having financial freedom, you can pursue your passions and live the life you want to live.

5   Reduced stress and anxiety

Finally, saving money can reduce your stress and anxiety. Money-related stress can have a significant impact on your mental health, and saving money can help alleviate this stress. By having an emergency fund and retirement savings, you can feel more secure and less anxious about your financial future. Furthermore, by living within your means and saving money, you can avoid debt and the accompanying stress that comes with it.

In conclusion, saving money is essential for financial stability, achieving your financial goals, and living a comfortable life. By having an emergency fund, contributing to retirement savings, and living within your means, you can reduce stress and anxiety, achieve financial freedom, and pursue the life you want to live. Saving money is a fundamental financial skill that everyone should develop to ensure financial security in the future.

Chapter 2: Debt Reduction

Debt reduction is the process of paying off your debts and reducing your overall debt load. Debt can be a significant financial burden, and it can impact your financial stability, credit score, and overall quality of life. Therefore, reducing your debt can help you achieve financial freedom, reduce your stress, and improve your financial well-being. In this detailed response, we will explore the importance of debt reduction and the strategies you can use to reduce your debt.

1. Improve your credit score
Reducing your debt can improve your credit score, which is a critical factor in securing loans and credit. Your credit score is a numerical representation of your creditworthiness, and it's used by lenders to determine whether you're a good candidate for a loan or credit. A higher credit score can lead to lower interest rates on loans and credit cards, saving you money in the long run. By reducing your debt load, you can improve your credit utilization ratio, which is a key factor in determining your credit score.

2.   Reduce stress

Debt can be a significant source of stress, and it can impact your mental health and overall quality of life. By reducing your debt load, you can reduce your stress levels and improve your overall well-being. Debt can lead to constant worry and anxiety, and reducing it can provide a sense of relief and peace of mind. By taking control of your debt and developing a debt reduction plan, you can regain control of your finances and reduce your stress levels.

3.   Save money

Reducing your debt can save you money in the long run. Debt comes with interest charges, and the longer you carry a balance, the more interest you'll pay over time. By reducing your debt load, you can save money on interest charges and reduce your overall debt payments. This extra money can then be used to invest, save for retirement, or achieve other financial goals.

4. Achieve financial freedom
Reducing your debt can also help you achieve financial freedom. Debt can be a significant burden on your finances, and it can limit your ability to pursue your financial goals. By reducing your debt load, you can free up your cash flow and create more financial flexibility. This can help you save for retirement, start a business, or pursue other opportunities that can lead to financial freedom.

5. Strategies for debt reduction

There are several strategies you can use to reduce your debt. One of the most effective strategies is the debt snowball method, where you focus on paying off your smallest debts first while making the minimum payments on your larger debts. As you pay off your smaller debts, you can use the extra money to pay off your larger debts, which can help you make significant progress in reducing your debt load.

Another strategy is the debt avalanche method, where you focus on paying off your debts with the highest interest rates first. This can help you save money on interest charges and reduce your overall debt load more quickly.

You can also consider consolidating your debts with a personal loan or a balance transfer credit card. This can help you simplify your debt payments and potentially reduce your interest rates, making it easier to pay off your debts.

In conclusion, reducing your debt is critical for achieving financial stability and freedom. By reducing your debt load, you can improve your credit score, reduce stress, save money, and achieve financial freedom. By developing a debt reduction plan and using effective strategies such as the debt snowball or debt avalanche method, you can take control of your debt and achieve your financial goals.

Chapter 3: Building an Emergency Fund

Building an emergency fund is an essential aspect of personal finance. An emergency fund is a savings account that is set aside for unexpected expenses, such as a job loss, medical emergency, or major car repair. The purpose of an emergency fund is to provide a financial safety net to help you weather unexpected expenses and financial setbacks without relying on credit cards or loans. In this detailed response, we will explore the importance of building an emergency fund and the strategies you can use to start building one.

Financial stability
Having an emergency fund can provide financial stability in times of uncertainty. Life is unpredictable, and unexpected expenses can occur at any time. Having an emergency fund can help you feel more secure about your finances and give you peace of mind in the face of unexpected expenses.

2.   Avoiding debt

Having an emergency fund can help you avoid going into debt when unexpected expenses arise. Without an emergency fund, you may have to rely on credit cards or loans to cover unexpected expenses, which can lead to high-interest payments and a cycle of debt. By having an emergency fund, you can avoid going into debt and save money in the long run.

3. Protecting your financial goals

An emergency fund can protect your financial goals and prevent setbacks. Unexpected expenses can disrupt your financial plans, such as saving for retirement, paying off debt, or buying a home. By having an emergency fund, you can protect your financial goals and prevent setbacks, allowing you to stay on track with your long-term financial plans.

4. How to start building an emergency fund

The first step in building an emergency fund is to set a savings goal. A good rule of thumb is to save enough to cover 3 to 6 months of living expenses. This may seem like a daunting task, but it's important to start small and gradually build your savings over time.

The next step is to create a budget and identify areas where you can reduce expenses. This can include cutting back on discretionary spending, negotiating bills, or finding ways to increase your income. Every little bit helps, and even small savings can add up over time.

Once you have identified areas where you can save, set up an automatic savings plan to transfer money into your emergency fund each month. This can be done through your employer's direct deposit or through your bank's automatic transfer feature.

5. How to maintain an emergency fund

After you have built your emergency fund, it's important to maintain it. This means avoiding the temptation to dip into your emergency fund for non-emergency expenses and replenishing your fund if you do have to use it.

One way to maintain your emergency fund is to regularly review your budget and adjust your savings goals if necessary. This can help ensure that you are always saving enough to cover unexpected expenses.

Another way to maintain your emergency fund is to invest your savings in a high-yield savings account or money market account. This can help you earn interest on your savings while keeping your money easily accessible in case of an emergency.

In conclusion, building an emergency fund is essential for financial stability and security. By setting a savings goal, creating a budget, and setting up an automatic savings plan, you can start building your emergency fund and protecting your financial well-being. Remember to maintain your emergency fund by avoiding non-emergency expenses and regularly reviewing your budget and savings goals.

Chapter 4: Investing Basics

Investing is the act of putting money into assets with the expectation of generating profit or income in the future. Investing can be a great way to grow your wealth over time, but it's important to understand the basics before you get started. In this detailed response, we will explore the fundamentals of investing, including the diffcrent types of investments, the risks involved, and the strategies you can use to start investing.

There are many types of investments available, and each has its own benefits and risks. Some common types of investments include

- Stocks: Stocks represent ownership in a company, and their value can go up or down depending on the company's performance and the broader market conditions.
- Bonds: Bonds are a type of debt instrument issued by companies or governments to raise funds. They typically pay a fixed interest rate and have a maturity date when the principal is repaid.
- Mutual Funds: Mutual funds are investment vehicles that pool money from multiple investors to invest in a diversified portfolio of stocks, bonds, or other assets.
- Exchange-Traded Funds (ETFs): ETFs are similar to mutual funds but trade like stocks on an exchange. They offer diversification and lower costs than actively managed mutual funds.
- Real Estate: Real estate can be a tangible investment that generates income through rent or capital appreciation over time.

Investing always involves some level of risk. It's important to understand the risks involved with each type of investment before you start investing. Some common risks include

- Market Risk: The risk that the value of your investments will decrease due to market fluctuations or changes in economic conditions.
- Credit Risk: The risk that the issuer of a bond will default on its payments.
- Inflation Risk: The risk that inflation will erode the purchasing power of your investments over time.
- Liquidity Risk: The risk that you won't be able to sell your investments when you need to due to a lack of buyers in the market.

1. Strategies for Investing

There are many strategies for investing, and the best approach will depend on your individual goals and risk tolerance. Some common strategies include

- Diversification: Diversifying your investments across different asset classes and sectors can help reduce risk and increase potential returns.
- Dollar-Cost Averaging: Investing a fixed amount of money at regular intervals can help reduce the impact of market fluctuations and average out the cost of your investments over time.
- Buy and Hold: Holding your investments for the long-term can help ride out market fluctuations and potentially generate higher returns over time.
- Active vs. Passive Investing: Active investing involves selecting individual stocks or other assets based on market analysis, while passive investing involves investing in index funds or ETFs that track a broad market index.

4.   Getting Started

Before you start investing, it's important to have a solid financial foundation in place. This includes paying off high-interest debt, building an emergency fund, and creating a budget. Once you have a solid financial foundation, you can start investing by opening a brokerage account and selecting your investments based on your goals and risk tolerance.

It's important to do your research and understand the risks involved before you start investing. Consider consulting with a financial advisor to help guide you through the process and develop a personalized investment strategy.

In conclusion, investing is a great way to grow your wealth over time, but it's important to understand the basics before you get started. Understanding the different types of investments, the risks involved, and the strategies for investing can help you make informed decisions and achieve your financial goals.

Chapter 5: Stocks & Bonds

Stocks and bonds are two of the most common types of investments available to investors. While they both represent ways to invest in a company or entity, they differ in their risk profiles, returns, and other characteristics. In this detailed response, we will explore the basics of stocks and bonds, including what they are, their benefits and risks, and how to invest in them.

1.   What are Stocks?
Stocks, also known as equities, represent ownership in a company. When you buy a share of stock, you become a shareholder in the company and are entitled to a portion of the company's earnings and assets. The value of a stock is determined by the performance of the company and the supply and demand in the market.

Investing in stocks can offer the potential for high returns, but it also comes with a higher level of risk. Stocks can be volatile and their prices can fluctuate greatly based on changes in the market or the company's performance. However, investing in a diversified portfolio of stocks can help to reduce risk and potentially generate higher returns over time.

2. What are Bonds?

Bonds are debt securities issued by corporations, governments, or other entities to raise funds. When you buy a bond, you are essentially loaning money to the issuer, who promises to pay you back with interest at a future date. Bonds typically offer lower returns than stocks, but they also come with lower risk.

Bonds are typically less volatile than stocks, and they offer a predictable stream of income through regular interest payments. They are often considered a safer investment than stocks, but their returns may not keep pace with inflation over time.

3. Benefits and Risk of Stocks and Bonds

The benefits and risks of stocks and bonds vary depending on the individual investor's goals and risk tolerance. Here are some general benefits and risks associated with each type of investment

Benefits of Stocks:
- Potential for higher returns over the long-term
- Ability to participate in a company's growth and success
- Potential for dividends and other income streams

Risks of Stocks:
- High level of volatility and risk
- Possibility of losing some or all of your investment
- Potential for market downturns and economic downturns

Benefits of Bonds:

- Lower risk compared to stocks
- Predictable stream of income through interest payments
- Ability to diversify your portfolio

Risks of Bonds:

- Lower returns compared to stocks
- Possibility of issuer defaulting on payments
- Risk of inflation eroding the value of your investment over time

1. How to Invest in Stocks and Bonds

Investing in stocks and bonds requires opening an investment account with a brokerage firm. Most online brokerages offer a wide range of investment options, including stocks, bonds, mutual funds, and exchange-traded funds (ETFs).

When investing in stocks, it's important to do your research and consider factors such as the company's financial health, growth prospects, and industry trends. Diversifying your portfolio across multiple stocks and sectors can help to reduce risk and increase potential returns over the long-term.

When investing in bonds, it's important to consider factors such as the issuer's credit rating, interest rate, and maturity date. Bond mutual funds or ETFs can offer a diversified portfolio of bonds and reduce risk compared to investing in individual bonds.

In conclusion, stocks and bonds are two of the most common types of investments available to investors. While they differ in their risk profiles, returns, and other characteristics, they can both play an important role in a diversified investment portfolio. It's important to understand the benefits and risks of each type of investment and to consult with a financial advisor to develop a personalized investment strategy that aligns with your goals and risk tolerance.

Chapter 6: Real Estate

Real estate is a term used to describe property consisting of land and the buildings or other improvements on it. Real estate is a tangible asset that can be owned, bought, sold, rented or leased for a variety of purposes. Real estate can be used for residential, commercial, industrial, or agricultural purposes.

Investing in real estate can be an attractive option for many investors. Real estate can provide both income and capital appreciation, and can also offer certain tax benefits. However, investing in real estate also comes with risks and challenges, and requires careful consideration and planning.

1.   Types of Real Estate Investments

There are several types of real estate investments, each with its own unique characteristics and potential benefits and risks

Residential Real Estate: This includes single-family homes, townhouses, condos, and multifamily apartment buildings. Investing in residential real estate can provide steady income through rent, and potential capital appreciation through property value appreciation.

Commercial Real Estate: This includes office buildings, retail spaces, warehouses, and other commercial properties. Investing in commercial real estate can provide steady income through rent and long-term leases, as well as potential capital appreciation through property value appreciation.

Industrial Real Estate: This includes manufacturing facilities, distribution centers, and other industrial properties. Investing in industrial real estate can provide steady income through rent and long-term leases, as well as potential capital appreciation through property value appreciation.

Raw Land: This includes undeveloped land that may be used for future development, such as building homes or commercial properties. Investing in raw land can provide potential capital appreciation through property value appreciation.

2. Benefits and Risks of Real Estate Investments

The benefits and risks of real estate investments depend on the type of investment and the specific property. Here are some general benefits and risks associated with investing in real estate

Benefits of Real Estate Investments:

- Steady income through rent or long-term leases
- Potential for capital appreciation through property value appreciation
- Potential tax benefits, such as deductions for property taxes and mortgage interest
- Potential to leverage other people's money through mortgages or other financing options

Risks of Real Estate Investments:

- High upfront costs, such as down payments and closing costs
- Maintenance and repair costs can be significant
- Property value can fluctuate based on economic conditions, market demand, and other factors
- Potential for vacancies, which can impact income and cash flow

1. How to Invest in Real Estate

Investing in real estate requires careful planning and research. Here are some general steps to consider when investing in real estate

- Define your investment goals: Determine your investment goals and risk tolerance, and decide which type of real estate investment aligns best with your goals.
- Research the market: Conduct research on the real estate market and trends, and identify potential properties or markets that align with your goals.
- Secure financing: Explore financing options, such as mortgages or other loans, to fund your investment.
- Conduct due diligence: Perform thorough due diligence on the property, including inspections, appraisals, and title searches.
- Manage the property: Once you have acquired the property, manage it effectively to maximize income and cash flow.
- Monitor and adjust: Continuously monitor your investment and adjust your strategy as needed to align with market conditions and your investment goals.

In conclusion, real estate can be an attractive investment option for many investors. Real estate can provide both income and capital appreciation, and can also offer certain tax benefits. However, investing in real estate also comes with risks and challenges, and requires careful consideration and planning. It's important to understand the benefits and risks of real estate investments, and to consult with a financial advisor or real estate professional to develop a personalized investment strategy that aligns with your goals and risk tolerance.

Chapter 7: Gold and Silver

Gold and silver are often seen as safe haven investments during times of economic uncertainty. They can provide a hedge against inflation and currency devaluation. However, investing in gold and silver also comes with risks, such as market fluctuations and storage costs.

To invest in gold and silver, you can buy physical bullion, such as coins or bars, or invest in exchange-traded funds (ETFs) that track the price of gold or silver. When investing in gold and silver, it's important to consider factors such as purity, weight, and storage options.

Chapter 8: Other Financial Assets

In addition to stocks, bonds, real estate, gold, and silver, there are many other types of financial assets you can invest in. These include mutual funds, exchange-traded funds, options, futures, and cryptocurrencies.

Mutual funds and ETFs are good options for those looking for a diversified portfolio. They allow you to invest in a range of assets, such as stocks and bonds, without having to buy each asset individually.

Options and futures are more complex financial assets that allow you to bet on the future price of a stock or commodity. These investments come with higher risks and require a deeper understanding of the market.

Cryptocurrencies, such as Bitcoin, are a relatively new investment option that has gained popularity in recent years. Cryptocurrencies are decentralized digital currencies that operate independently of banks and governments. However, they also come with high volatility and regulatory uncertainty.

Chapter 9: Putting it All Together

To achieve financial freedom, having a well-rounded investment strategy that includes a mix of different assets is important. This means diversifying your portfolio across stocks, bonds, real estate, and other financial assets.

It's also important to have a long-term investment strategy that focuses on your goals and risk tolerance. This means creating a plan and sticking to it, even during times of market volatility. It's also important to review and adjust your investment strategy regularly to ensure that it remains aligned with your goals.

Conclusion

Saving money and investing wisely can be the key to achieving financial freedom. By following the steps outlined in this book, you can create a solid financial plan that includes budgeting, debt reduction, emergency funds, and a well-diversified investment portfolio. Remember, build wealth